Kernels of Knowledge

Change Your Thinking, Change Your Life

By: Morgan

ISBN: 1515310396
ISBN 13: 9781515310396
Library of Congress Control Number: 2015912598
CreateSpace Independent Publishing Platform
North Charleston, South Carolina

INTRODUCTION

Change your thinking, change your life! Kernels of Knowledge shows you how to take complete control of your mind and focus your mental powers on any goal.

—BRIAN TRACY, AUTHOR, *THE POWER OF SELF-CONFIDENCE*

*K*ERNELS OF *K*NOWLEDGE provides a road map of how to crawl inside your own head and walks you through a process designed to determine where you are, where you want to go, and how you can get there. It utilizes thought-provoking and sometimes humorous quotes, a pinch of life stories, a dash of poetry, and two parts practical and proven advice. It delves into the creative power of thoughts and dreams and reveals how, when that power is carefully harnessed, you can eliminate your fears, define your goals, and make your dreams come true. There is a fine line between insanity and brilliance as you journey through your mind and not only talk but also sometimes debate with your own internal experts. These kernels of knowledge walk you through the baby steps that will lead you from thoughts to dreams, from dreams to action steps, and from action steps to your reality.

I am president of the Morgan Group, Inc. (www.morgangroup-dev.com), a residential real-estate development company. The Morgan Group website will provide you with my professional background and accomplishments, which include more than thirty years of experience in the acquisition, financing, development, and disposition of assets acquired through various companies, partnerships, and joint ventures. The principles acquired through the life lessons outlined in this book are the basis that can enable you to achieve success in your professional life. I have been a real-estate entrepreneur for most of my career. More importantly, these valuable lessons I've attained are not restricted to your professional world; they're equally transferable to your personal life.

My educational credentials include a BA in communication arts from Michigan State University, where I played on the 1965 and 1966 national-championship football teams. Please note that, in my case, my athletic accomplishments are as important as my educational credentials. While I am certainly not downplaying the value and benefits received from the formal training of the mind, the kernels of knowledge attained through playing sports include leadership, teamwork, developing a game plan, dedication, hard work, and knowing your opponent's strengths and weaknesses as well as your own. These assets are all derived through participation in athletics but not necessarily in the classroom.

So what's more important—your education or your experience? Both are equally important, and the right combination is essential. My entrepreneurial life has been filled with adventure, change, and the risk of stepping into the unknown. Education prepares your mind for how to think, but your experience directs your mind as to what to think about. Your mind needs direction. The objective of this book is to provide that direction.

Inspiration is disguised in mysterious ways. My inspiration for writing this book was a rare opportunity to spend some quality time with my ninety-two-year-old mother-in-law prior to her death. In her final days, we were able to revisit her life lessons that she wished to pass on to her family. We produced an emotional CD entitled *Good-bye* that included those lessons she wished to leave behind for her family. While I benefited

INTRODUCTION

Change your thinking, change your life! Kernels of Knowledge shows you how to take complete control of your mind and focus your mental powers on any goal.

—BRIAN TRACY, AUTHOR, *THE POWER OF SELF-CONFIDENCE*

KERNELS OF KNOWLEDGE provides a road map of how to crawl inside your own head and walks you through a process designed to determine where you are, where you want to go, and how you can get there. It utilizes thought-provoking and sometimes humorous quotes, a pinch of life stories, a dash of poetry, and two parts practical and proven advice. It delves into the creative power of thoughts and dreams and reveals how, when that power is carefully harnessed, you can eliminate your fears, define your goals, and make your dreams come true. There is a fine line between insanity and brilliance as you journey through your mind and not only talk but also sometimes debate with your own internal experts. These kernels of knowledge walk you through the baby steps that will lead you from thoughts to dreams, from dreams to action steps, and from action steps to your reality.

I am president of the Morgan Group, Inc. (www.morgangroup-dev.com), a residential real-estate development company. The Morgan Group website will provide you with my professional background and accomplishments, which include more than thirty years of experience in the acquisition, financing, development, and disposition of assets acquired through various companies, partnerships, and joint ventures. The principles acquired through the life lessons outlined in this book are the basis that can enable you to achieve success in your professional life. I have been a real-estate entrepreneur for most of my career. More importantly, these valuable lessons I've attained are not restricted to your professional world; they're equally transferable to your personal life.

My educational credentials include a BA in communication arts from Michigan State University, where I played on the 1965 and 1966 national-championship football teams. Please note that, in my case, my athletic accomplishments are as important as my educational credentials. While I am certainly not downplaying the value and benefits received from the formal training of the mind, the kernels of knowledge attained through playing sports include leadership, teamwork, developing a game plan, dedication, hard work, and knowing your opponent's strengths and weaknesses as well as your own. These assets are all derived through participation in athletics but not necessarily in the classroom.

So what's more important—your education or your experience? Both are equally important, and the right combination is essential. My entrepreneurial life has been filled with adventure, change, and the risk of stepping into the unknown. Education prepares your mind for how to think, but your experience directs your mind as to what to think about. Your mind needs direction. The objective of this book is to provide that direction.

Inspiration is disguised in mysterious ways. My inspiration for writing this book was a rare opportunity to spend some quality time with my ninety-two-year-old mother-in-law prior to her death. In her final days, we were able to revisit her life lessons that she wished to pass on to her family. We produced an emotional CD entitled *Good-bye* that included those lessons she wished to leave behind for her family. While I benefited emotionally from this labor of love, this tragic event inspired me to write *Kernels of Knowledge* to benefit you in your quest to define what it is you want to do when you "grow up," how to achieve it, and how to find happiness in the journey.

CONTENTS

MEETINGS WITH MYSELF

A FEW YEARS BACK, I created a self-evaluation system based on the following questions: "Where am I?" "Where do I want to go?" and "What do I have to do to get there?" Answer these three questions and dedicate yourself to the achievement of these goals, and you will be happy for the rest of your life.

My "Meetings with Myself" were always interesting and entertaining; they allowed me to evaluate whether I was moving in the right direction. It's one of those mind games that are best performed alone.

Find a place of solitude. Look into the distance and into the future. Visualize the tomorrow you are going to build, and begin to build that tomorrow today.

—Jonathan Lockwood Huie, author of Philosopher of Happiness

You might want to sit in a yoga position, with legs crossed and palms open, and give in to the energy around you. Or you might want to do what I do—just relax, make yourself comfortable, and get ready for an enlightening journey. Turn off the computers and the iPhone, as you will be going to a place that they can never understand. Find a quiet place, relax, and take yourself into your fantasy world, surrounded with silence and peace, away from your chaotic life. Music is optional.

Man is a slow, sloppy, and brilliant thinker; the machine is fast, accurate, and stupid.

—William M. Kelly

As Rhonda Byrne writes in her book *The Secret*, the law of attraction indicates you can control what you think and believe. I do not presume to understand how the mind works; however, if you are able to tap into this power of your inner thoughts and learn to control what you think, then you can better direct and control not only what happens in your life but also the results.

I'm not sure that "If I believe, if I just think it," it will magically happen—I'm just a kid from Ohio who used to play football. So when we start talking about "visualizations," "inner seeing," and vibrations that are transferred into the atmosphere, I get a little lost. But what I do know and adamantly support is that if you believe in your thoughts and focus on those things you need to change, you can make it happen. If you can learn to control and formulate what you think in a logical sequence and transfer those thoughts into your dreams and actions, then anything is possible.

What we are today comes from our thoughts of yesterday, and our present thoughts build our lives of tomorrow.

—Buddha

This Meeting with Myself exercise is independent, unabashed, and uncensored. It has a few rules and boundaries that allow for truthful self-evaluation of where you are, where you want to go, and how best to achieve those goals. The entire process is designed around careful and creative thoughts and dreams.

You have the power to control your mind, to visualize, and to evaluate. This allows you to look inside your head and plant the seeds of thoughts and dreams that, when cultivated, can define, grow, and provide you direction.

The mind is a powerful ally of the brain. Your brain is your own built-in three-pound computer, made up of 100 billion neurons that regulates all physical aspects of your body—from heartbeat to blood pressure, from nerves to breathing, from taste to smell. Your *mind*, however, is not limited to physical functions; it also encompasses the emotional power within you.

Dr. Daniel Siegel, a professor of psychiatry at UCLA School of Medicine, in his book, *Mindsight: The New Science of Personal Transformation*, identifies the relationship between our brains and our minds as a "powerful lens through which we can understand our inner lives with more clarity, integrate the brain, and enhance our relationships with others. Mindsight is a kind of focused attention that allows us to see the internal workings of our own minds. It helps us get ourselves off of the autopilot of ingrained behaviors and habitual responses. It lets us 'name and tame' the emotions we are experiencing, rather than being overwhelmed by them."

Dr. Siegel dispels the notion of the old saying "Talking with yourself is OK so long as you don't talk back." You can call it whatever you want—meditation, self-talk, or Meetings with Myself—but this all-important journey through your mind helps formulate your direction and crystallizes your plans.

He who knows others is wise; he who knows himself is enlightened.
—Lao Tzu, Chinese author

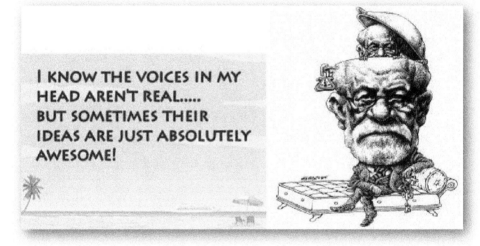

Psychologists indicate that talking with yourself is perfectly normal and can have a great deal of emotional benefit that contradicts the idea "What can we tell ourselves that we don't already know?" It helps to focus and clarify your thoughts and evaluate and confirm your decisions. Dr. Charles Chio states in his article published in Live Science magazine, "Talking to Yourself may Boost Brainpower", indicates that "Talking to yourself might not mean you are crazy—it can actually benefit thinking and perception." It's always beneficial to talk through your problem by having a serious dialogue with yourself in the privacy of your own mind, and be sure to consult with all of the voices in your head, your own mental board of directors—the dreamer, the accountant, the pessimist, the deal junkie, the marketing person, the lawyer, and whoever else has been invited to your meeting.

Your inner voice is subtle but grows stronger when you listen.

—Unknown

Your meetings have only a few rules:

1. Find a quiet place.
2. Do not allow any interruptions.
3. Take only brief notes to avoid disruptions of the creative process.

These conversations will be documented and incorporated into your game plan in chapter 2.

The sequence of the questions is important, as you need to know your starting point prior to attempting to establish where you want to go. You would think that determining "How do I get there?" would be the most difficult question; however, you will learn that "Where do I want to go?" actually requires the most imagination, is the most difficult to visualize, and is the most important to your success. It entails looking inside your soul to determine what you want to do when you grow up—a tall order. Growing up is when you take that first step into our new world and find out who you are, lose the illusions of youth, and discover the world of choices. There is no predetermined age that this miracle is discovered; it might be twenty or forty...or never.

When work, commitment, and pleasure all become one and you reach that deep well where passion lives, nothing is impossible.

—Anonymous

This exercise requires passion, assessment, and concentration, with a dash of realism. Once the "where" becomes evident, the "how" is easier to identify, schedule, and achieve.

If you don't know where you want to go, most any road will get you there.

—Lewis Carroll, English author of Alice's Adventures in Wonderland

WHERE AM I?

"Where am I?" generally takes the stage first. Evaluate each of the projects or relationships you are involved with, and recap the issues and decisions you've made, as well as any changes that you were required to implement. You must look in the mirror and deal with your current realities. The "Where am I?" agenda is a review of your current situation and entails more of an administrative review or highlight of the existing facts—what you have been able to accomplish and why, along with what your pending issues are and their current statuses.

WHERE DO I WANT TO GO?

The "Where do I want to go?" follows this evaluation. This is the most fun and also the most important of all your objectives. You need to realize that in order for this session to truly be productive, you need to tell the pessimist in you to sit down and shut up—he or she will never believe your dreams are possible. I also like to make sure the "deal junkie" is in attendance, as he or she believe you can fly. This is your time to dream, and in your dream world, you can achieve anything you can conceive. While the pessimist's opinions are extremely important, he or she can rejoin you later and bring all his or her input in the "How do I get there?" session.

Vision is the art of seeing things invisible.

—Jonathan Swift, Anglo-Irish poet

It's important to raise the bar, to dream, and to picture yourself living in the world you wish to build. There are no boundaries; you are limited only by your imagination. Your career, love life, car, house, or money—it's all on the table. This session requires uninhibited imagination. In most cases, you might find that you hesitate to allow yourself to attempt to achieve your dreams and goals for fear of failure. You need to set those fears aside and just go for it!

It helps if you ask yourself where you want to be in one year, in five years, or even in ten years. It's difficult to determine the answer to "Where do I want to go?" but it's imperative that you do so. Evaluating the probabilities should be minimized, as you do not want to limit or discourage, but rather set yourself free to dream the impossible. Those negative thoughts will destroy the continuity of this session and will be discussed later in detail during the "How do I get there?" session. Be crystal clear as to your vision, dedicate yourself, and have belief in your ability to achieve it. Deadlines, obstacles, and roadblocks to achievement will all be evaluated later. Now is your time to dream. And never, ever let your fears prevent you from living your dream life.

The greater danger for most of us is not that our aim is too high and we miss it, but that it is too low and we reach it

—Michelangelo

I recently read an interesting article called "The Second Wave of Transformation," by John Mauldin. He outlines several compelling projections of how technology will change our lives in the next two decades, and we need to be aware of these changes and incorporate them into our future planning. One of Mr. Mauldin's intriguing projections, which is near and dear to our hearts, states, "We won't be physically immortal, but the things that kill most of us today will not be a problem. We will just get...older. And we will be able to repair a great deal of the damage from aging." Scientists are even "starting to print 3-D human organs," according to the article, and Mauldin also purports that "we will see more change in the next twenty years than we saw in the last one hundred!"

So the good news is that maybe—just maybe—you will live longer than you thought, but the bad news is that if you are not prepared, your financial world could be a disaster. As Michelangelo stated, "it might be better to aim too high and miss than aim too low and make it." It's important to keep this in mind and incorporate it into your "Where do I want to go?" and "How do I get there?" sessions.

We should also be aware that this session was researched by the "accountant." He or she understands that in the 1960s, there were one hundred thousand millionaires. It has been projected, however, that by the mid-twenty-first century, *all* professionals will be millionaires, according to observations by Burleson Consulting (www.burlesonconsulting.com). The percentage of millionaires in the United States will have increased from 3 percent of the population in 2007 (nine million) to approximately 20 percent of the population by 2050 (seventy million). Now, a loaf of bread might cost twenty dollars in 2050, but what this tells you is that you might want to raise the bar, because your financial world is changing. You need to take these facts into consideration in your Meetings with Myself.

Your Meetings with Myself is not a one-time process, but rather a continual exercise that should be scheduled periodically. In most cases, "Where do I want to go?" has been discussed and established early on, in previous meetings, as this is essential to your direction and affects the establishment of directional task from the onset; however, these objectives need to be continually revisited and updated as required. But more importantly, you need to continually reinforce your dreams and constantly monitor your progress.

HOW DO I GET THERE?

Finally we have the all-important "How do I get there?" session. Occasionally, you're required to make changes, and as author of your dream thoughts, you reserve the right and responsibility to initiate these adjustments as needed. Written synopsis, incorporated in the game plan in the next chapter, is essential, or you can get lost. The very acts of writing down your goal, formulating your plan, and transferring its steps to your to-do list embed in your mind the direction and guarantee the actions required to keep you on track to accomplish your goals.

You don't make decisions in a vacuum; they require input from those internal and external experts who have dealt with the issues, those who know the people and problems and deal with them every day. Healthy conflicts are inevitable—say, between the ego person in you, who wants to buy that big house, and the accountant in you, who says, "You're an idiot" (those unabashed, uncensored discussions we have within our minds).

Now, it's true you are talking with yourself—and some may view this as being a little crazy—but within us all, we have those bits of expertise that we call upon periodically when evaluating how we need to get where we want to go. For example, depending on the problem you are evaluating, you might recall the experience of the marketing person or the lawyer or the one I hate—the accountant—for inspiration prior to making decisions and formulating your plan.

Now, you may think this self-talk is a little crazy—and maybe it is, but you need to remember there is a thin line between brilliance and insanity.

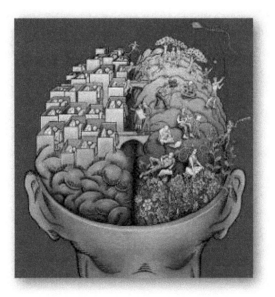

The point is that your mind and experiences allow you to evaluate the steps you need to take to determine the direction you have to go before implementing your best plan. Experience has taught us that while it's not a lot of fun talking with the accountant, as a general rule, he or she needs to sign off on all financial matters incorporated into the final plan.

Now, sometimes you make decisions on the spur of the moment, and sometimes that works. I'm just saying that decisions will work better and be successful more often if you have thought about them first. You can make better decisions with better results if you debate them before your board of directors.

The "How do I get there?" meeting requires that each thought be developed into specific goals and steps that require action, so set the beer down, and let's get to work. This is where the rubber meets the road. All those grand plans can't be achieved without documenting and setting time frames for those tasks, ones that clearly describe "How do I get there?"

You have crawled inside your head, and only you can clearly define those goals you have set up for yourself. It reminds me of a story about a project manager who was talking with one of his ambitious, overachieving team members. As he laid out those tasks that needed to be done, the overachiever continually answered, "I can do that!" to all the assignments. But later, after the meeting, in the quiet of his own office, the team member said to himself, "Oh, shit. How am I going to do all that?" The same is true with the goals that you've established in the "Where do I want to go?" segment of your meetings. Now you need to determine the "how."

First, you need to clearly articulate to yourself on paper exactly what you have determined your goals to be. If you are like me in the "Where do I want to go?" session, you would have got a little crazy and were carried away. This is when you need to bring in the administration person and call upon his or her expertise to organize all the craziness. In other words, you need to organize your thoughts.

Now, please don't think that the "crazy" I'm talking about is truly crazy, because crazy sits directly on that line between insanity and brilliance. So brilliance or insanity—I don't know, you decide.

This is the time when you, as the chairman of the board, call in all your internal experts. You need to bring back the pessimist, the accountant, the lawyer—the whole team. How you document this is up to you, but my administrative person likes to break it down into two categories: personal (health, relationships, family, friends, self-esteem, respect, attitude, love, freedom, and all the other things money can't buy), and financial (income, house, car, travel, and all the other things money can buy).

I think it's important to realize that happiness and success are not always about money. There are good reasons why "personal" is listed first. The principles outlined in this book are equally transferable to both. Too often we interpret a motivational or a self-help book as dealing primarily with our financial world and secondarily to our health, love, respect, relationships, and self-esteem. Happiness is achieved through a coordinated balance of the two. Being financially secure without good health doesn't work well. To have money without love is empty. Money without family and friends or respect doesn't mean much, either.

A high priority on my list is to play a part in the lives of my children and my grandchildren. A few years ago, I read an inspirational book by Mac Anderson and Lance Wubbels called *To a Child Love Is Spelled T-I-M-E*. It features a story about a father who takes off work to go fishing with his son. Years later, he reads through his daily journals and comes across his note for that day: "Wasted all day…took Johnny fishing, didn't catch anything." He notices he also has Johnny's diary, so he checks to see what Johnny wrote about that day. Johnny's diary reads, "Spent time with Dad, went fishing, and it was the greatest day of my life!" Think about this in establishing the priority of your dreams.

Each goal, whether personal or financial, requires a clear, brief statement as to your objective. Additionally, it requires those specific tasks that are needed to achieve your goals and a time frame for attaining them.

One example of my dream playing a part in the lives of my children and my children's children was when my wife and I established "Kids Camp." Each year, we invite all children, young and old (as we are all kids at heart), to spend the weekend at our Michigan home, playing in the swimming hole, having water wars, stargazing, and holding a fishing contest, fish fry, and corn fest. Besides being a great time, the annual bonding is amazing, and the memories will last forever.

Change how a person thinks and you will change how they feel.
Change how they feel, and you will change how they perform.
Change how they perform, and you will change the results. Change
the results and you will change their life.

—R. W. Ross

Your entire game plan evolves as you walk through this process. Sometimes the pessimist is right. Sometimes the accountant will determine that your goal needs refining. Sometimes the doctor is like a broken record telling you, "Lose weight. Lose weight." And sometimes the love of your life breaks your heart.

Your internal experts have their limitations, and in many cases they require outside counsel. The accountant periodically enlists the expertise of a CPA, bank, or investors. The creative person may consult with the professional architect, the constructor may consult with the engineer, and the lawyer may spend a lot of time with the attorney. The "how" requires a continual search for input through and cooperation from the outside world.

"How do I get there?" sometimes requires finding a mentor. Seek advice or sign up for that class that you've been putting off for the last five years. As the Nike ads say, just do it! Don't be afraid to ask for help. Your contact list is a powerful tool. Use it!

I want to tell you a story that I heard from John Lawrence, an author and career counselor. A friend's son asked John for his advice. The young man had been accepted to Harvard and, at the other end of the spectrum, also Ball State University, a small college located in Muncie, Indiana. He was impressed with the idea of a degree from Harvard. However, the cost difference was about $40,000 per year. John's recommendation to this student, who wanted to work in the motion picture business, and his father was: go to Ball State. It has a very good communications department for theater, art, and film. Then, with the money he saved by not going to Harvard, he could spend the entire summer in Los Angeles, working in the film industry as an unpaid intern. This invaluable experience and contacts that would be realized would go a long way in offsetting the prestige of a degree from Harvard.

I guess what I'm saying is that some sort of combination of experience and education is the ultimate goal. Find a way to add to your education and generate contacts that could give you an introduction to the business as well as put you at the front of the line when looking for a job once you graduate. A good mentor is priceless on your journey to finding your dreams.

The evolution of your dreams is continuous, and flexibility is required. The roadmap outlined in the next chapter, "Game Plan," will provide the step-by-step guidelines to take you from where you are to where you want to be. Please understand that, when completed, this becomes the most important document in the world to you, so treat it accordingly.

Meeting with Myself

Periodic meetings to know where you are at,
To confirm the right road and direct your internal chat.
Between insanity and brilliance is a fine line.
Both require thinking outside the box and in your mind.

It refreshes your direction and defines your role.
It brightens your objectives and describes your soul.
Agendas work best so that you don't lose track,
To point out where you want to go and what you lack.

To remember where you are at and want to go,
And rehashing the how, is nice to know.

Knowing "Where do I want to go?" is your ultimate goal.
Reach inside your soul and be prepared to pay the toll.

While the "How do I get there?" is always hard.
You have the tools, so just pick the right card.
In order to be meaningful, you direct your action.
Document your steps to increase your traction.

There are many areas of expertise within your mind.
This knowledge is called upon many, many times.
Maybe it's legal or financial, or maybe the creative girl or guy.
They are all present and continually question, "Why?"

You are compromised by the inner voices in your head.
You listen and learn by what is said
During the private conversations among your many selves
As they discuss your options to determine what sells.

Sometimes you need decisions and sometimes not
Each has his or her opinion, and sometimes things get hot
As you continue to evaluate and strive to compress,
Your Meetings with Myself will increase your success.

—Morgan

Game Plan

PERIODICALLY, I HAVE requests to mentor individuals who are searching to find the answers to what do I want to do? Now these individuals come in all shapes and forms: men, women, young, and old. These requests are primarily for the purpose of establishing a game plan for their potential future entrepreneurial endeavors, as that's where majority of my kernels of knowledge reside.

The game plan can only be initiated once you have determined in your "Meeting with Myself" what your dreams and goal are. This exercise culminates with the completion of the all-important game plan that can convert your personal and professional efforts toward achieving your dreams and goals.

It's important to point out that the examples outlined might pertain to real estate; however, these same kernels of knowledge apply to whatever field you might chose. Whether you are looking for a job, attempting to get a promotion, planning to start your own company, selling that big deal, or winning the heart of that special person, you need to have a game plan that can assist in walking you through your maze of options. A road-map that simplifies and provides direction through life's twists and turns that can get you from point "A" (where you are) to point "B" (where you want to be).

Life sometimes provides you with directional challenges that are a little more complicated than go straight on Main Street and take a left on State, as depicted below in the Dallas, Texas freeway interchange. I can pretty much guarantee that if you don't have a plan, you *will* get lost.

Freeway Interchange, Dallas, Texas

Jack Canfield, author of *Chicken Soup for the Soul* and a motivational speaker, in his commencement speech at Harvard, told a story about Lou Holtz, a football coach for seven different universities throughout his career with an overall record of 249–132–7, including the 1988 Norte Dame National Championship. Early in his career, after he was fired from the University of South Carolina, his wife, Beth, gave him the book *The Magic of Thinking Big*, by David Schwartz. The book asks the reader to write down 101 goals he or she wishes to attain in life. Later his wife asked if he had read the book, and he said yes and showed her his bucket list of 101 items. After reading through the 101 things, which included river rafting on the Snake River, winning the national championship, meeting the pope and the president, touring the Great Wall of China, riding on a submarine, she looked at Lou and said, "There's one more thing you need to add...'Get a job!'" So you need to not only generate the game plan; you will need to prioritize it as well.

The game plan is essential to your success. Eason Ding and Tim Hursey wrote a report on the benefits of writing a business plan, with the supervision of Professor Joe Stone of the University of Oregon Department of Economics. Ding and Hursey's analysis concluded that writing a business plan doubled the success rate in every one of the goals outlined in the report. A business plan is essentially the same as your game plan, so if your goal is to be successful, then there is no better way to insure your success than to write the plan!

A goal without a plan is just a wish.
—Antoine de Saint-Exupéry, author of The Little Prince

To effectively walk you through the process, I have generated an example of a game plan so that the outline has more definition and substance.

For the purpose of this evaluation, I am creating a fictional character; let's call him Maxwell. Maxwell is twenty-seven years old. He was a college graduate and an average student. He is happily married to Suzie and they have a son, Max. He is working for a small real-estate developer that owns and manages several rental apartments, and oversees the construction of single family homes and the development of a twenty-unit condominium project. Maxwell oversees construction, management, secures loans, sales, marketing, and the closing process. The owner identifies the opportunities, raises the capital, and guarantees the financing. Maxwell enjoys his work and has established a great relationship with his boss, whom he also considers his mentor. In his "Meetings with Myself," Maxwell has articulated his dreams and set his goals to start his own real-estate development firm.

This game plan covers your personal and profession goals that spell out how he was going to achieve and make his dreams come true. You need to keep in mind that any game plan requires continual revisions and updates on a regular basis. Additionally, we attain our dreams one small step at a time so that we can celebrate those small successes along the way.

Game Plan (*Fast-forward five years*)
Date: (*todays date plus 5 years*)
Five-Year Vision: Maxwell Properties is a successful real-estate development company specializing in the acquisition and redevelopment of distressed residential properties within the fringe neighborhood of Chicago. We (the Maxwell's) have an annual combined income of $275,000 and a net worth of $1 million and live in a beautiful four-thousand-square-foot, four-bedroom, and three-bath home that we acquired and renovated four years ago. Our son, Max Jr., attends the local highly rated charter school where my wife, Suzie Maxwell, is a teacher. Our daughter, Maggie, attends the preschool on Halsted Street. I am active within the community and coach little league baseball for the local team. Suzie is active on the school board, and both Suzie and I attend cooking classes on Tuesday evening at the local culinary institute. We enjoy a one-week family vacation, with this year's selection being Disney World. Suzie and I also have our annual romantic getaway somewhere that generally involves sun and a beach with a hammock.

Note:
The objective here is to paint the vision of where it is that you will be in five years, or ten years, from now and don't be afraid to dream. The ten-year plan really is a lot of fun, but for our present example we need to describe the "how" for the presented five-year plan. In the next section you will define how this plan will be implemented and the hurdles that need to be overcome. This is not meant to be an all-inclusive list but rather a synopsis, as much of the details will require a far more comprehensive analysis. (e.g., Maxwell Business Plan, which needs to be generated as a separate document.) The game plan is divided into two categories: personal and professional.

Personal

- **Health**: Lose twenty pounds (190 lbs.) by New Year's Day.

Action Steps:

1. Join health club and spend one hour four days a week exercising.
2. Diet by utilizing portion control and no snacks after evening meal.
- **Love**: Regain Life's passions that periodically gets lost from job pressures, kids, and stress.

Action Steps:

1. Date night once a month.
2. Plan this year's romantic vacation.
3. Suzie and I would like one more child (see 1 and 2 above).
- **Relationships**: Don't forget the important people in my life.

Action Steps:

1. Take Max on fishing charter in Michigan in July.
2. Call and visit my mother once a week.
3. Take Maggie and Max Jr. to Museum of Science & Industry, Children Museum, and Grant Park for the fireworks, coach, PTA.

Professional

There are some glaring shortcomings that I need to overcome, or master, to get from where I am to where I want to be. I will outline these deficiencies, together with my game plan to eliminate or diminish their ability to impede my progress. They are as follows:

- **Money:** To implement my plan I need capital or access to capital.

Action Steps:

1. Develop a detailed business plan for Maxwell Properties that clearly identifies the objectives, the market, the financing, and the people. It is to also include executive summary, mission statement, keys to success, ownership, market analysis, competition, strengths and weaknesses, marketing plan, and financial projection.(Note: There are a number of websites you can view that will walk you through this essential step. www.score.org/resources/business-plan-template-startup-business)
2. Find a financial partner who provides capital for a percentage of the deal.
   a. Plan A: Schedule a meeting with your boss and present a scenario whereby I take on more responsibilities of finding the properties, raising capital, and securing financing and joint guarantees of loans as a partner. (Note: this is a risk I need to be very careful with as it could blow up in my face.) If "No", proceed to Plan B.
   b. Plan B: Negotiate arrangement to allow me to proceed on my own while continuing as an employee. If "No" cautiously proceed to Plan C.
   c. Plan C: Complete existing projects and proceed on my own without the safety net of a guaranteed income.
3. Incomes are to be generated from several sources. Maxwell's income will increase to $275,000 during the five-year period, which includes Suzie's income as a teacher. Additionally, investment capital from profits will be generated.
4. Financial partners generally require the development partner to contribute at least 10 percent of the equity requirement. Establish

investment capital fund from real-estate commissions and development fees, which will be utilized for this purpose.

5. Investigate "cloud funding" as a potential money source.
6. Establish a group of potential "friends and family" investors and don't be shy. Be fair, be honest, and be careful. There is only one thing worse than losing money and that is losing money that was contributed by family or friends.

• **Knowledge** (knowledge brings credibility and respect)

Action Steps:

1. Secure my real-estate broker's license, which will allow for me to contribute fees to real-estate deals that I am able to generate.
2. Start the series of classes to attain my CCIM designation (Certified Commercial Investment Member). My knowledge is good, but I need to be better.
3. Become more efficient with the excel spreadsheet programs. Classes are available. Sign up immediately.

• **Properties**

Action Steps:

1. Finding the right property at the right price is hard. Odds are you will have to evaluate twenty properties to put one under contract and that does not guarantee I will close on it. Establish a working relationship with the following:
   a. REO (real-estate owned) departments of the three largest lenders
   b. Auction houses that deal in residential properties
   c. Three largest real-estate firms that deal with lenders' REOs

4. Locate and purchase bank-owned single family home for the use of the Maxwell family located in the near north neighborhood with good school system.

5. Close, develop, and/or renovate three properties each year for the next five years. Start with smaller properties in years one and two, with an increase in size as ability to finance increases.

6. Retain one property per year as a rental for cash flow and long-term appreciation and two properties will be developed for resale and immediate cash flow to augment acquisition program.

7. Prepare two presentation packages including everything from demographics, financial projections, construction costs, zoning issues, investment equity required, construction, and permanent financing on each project. Prepare one package for lender and one for investors outlining timing and investment return on equity.

- **Administrative**

Action Steps:

1. Contact a real-estate attorney and prepare the Limited Liability Corporation (LLC) and Investor Subscription Agreements.

2. Expand and coordinate team network to include an accountant, an attorney, constructors, salespeople, lenders, and investors. Join REIA (Real Estate Investment Association) and other networking groups to expand current network.

3. Develop Maxwell website.

- **Net Worth**

Action Steps:

1. A net worth of $1,000,000 based on value of property investment will be accumulated with the value and equity outlined in the

Maxwell Properties business plan. To establish a high net worth is essential to my financial security, but it becomes imperative for financing the implementation of my game plan (www.score.org/resources/business-plan-template-startup-business).

The example above is only meant to be a guideline and every dream is different, whether you are just getting into the job market, planning for that next promotion, or intending to find the love of your life. Getting from point "A" to point "B" is best achieved with a plan.

The game plan becomes a document that is a starting point to describe the action steps needed to get to where you want to go. To experience positive traction, you must transfer the action steps into your daily to-do list. If you formatted your game plan as shown above, then you are a leg up on 90 percent of the rest of the pack. Now there is nothing that can stop you but you. Your path is clear and your plan is laid, so take the action *now*!

I want one moment in time, when I'm more than I thought I could be, when all of my dreams are a heartbeat away and the answers are all up to me.

—Whitney Houston, "One Moment in Time"

Game Plan

A wish is a goal without a plan;
Review often to determine where you stand.

Write it down and check it twice.
Success depends on it, so be concise.

A plan provides the road to your dreams;
Follow the path and assemble your team.

When personal and professional goals are attained.
Celebrate those victories and break out the champagne.

Hard work and commitment go hand and hand.
Success is determined by following your game plan.

—Morgan

POWER OF THOUGHTS

THOUGHTS ARE LIKE magnetic pulses that go off in our brains, sometimes with explosive force. It's like lighting a pack of firecrackers and sitting back to watch how one thought explodes into the next and the next. When you brainstorm these thoughts, they have the power to generate directions, plans, and solutions. Thoughts are not facts. They are not concrete. They are intangible, they are private, and they are automatic. Once you open up this spigot of thought, you can just sit back and enjoy the ride.

Mountains of data, scientific research, and case studies have provided indisputable evidence that explains how the science of thoughts can be utilized to harness, direct, and understand how your thoughts can assist you in this journey to achieve a better life.

Tania Kotsos, PhD, is a doctor of philosophy from Athens University and the founder and author of Mind Your Reality (www.mind-your-reality.com). In her book *The Adventures of I*, she teaches how the power of your thoughts "enables and empowers you to understand as well as see, in a 'tangibly measurable' kind of way, what a profound and transformational difference your mind, the thoughts that flow through it, as well as the emotions that are ignited as a result of those thoughts, have in determining the kind and quality of *your* life." Everything in your world begins with the Power of Thought.

Without the Power of Thought, you have no power.
—Tania Kotsos, author and creator of Mind Your Reality

Uncontrolled, your thoughts can be either highly explosive, dangerous, or inspirationally powerful and life changing. A tremendous amount of evidence indicates that positive thoughts are more mentally powerful than negative thoughts and play an important part in molding your future. Positive thoughts generate positive actions, which translate into positive results. You have the option to dwell on those things that either produce positive thoughts or generate negative thoughts, as your mind doesn't distinguish the difference. It accepts and records whatever you present it. You alone have the ability to direct and control whether you choose a life filled with abundance, happiness, and prosperity or one of desperation, sadness, and despair.

Change your thoughts and you will change your world.
　　　—Tania Kotsos, author and creator of Mind Your Reality

When we change the way we look at things, the things we look at change.
　　　—Dr. Wayne Dyer, internationally renowned author

Your thoughts include the critical-thinking ability that enables you to apply rationality in identifying the real challenges you face and allows you to make better decisions, solve problems, and deal with change, thus producing much better results. The experts indicate that your thoughts are highly contagious—both in your own mind, just like the firecracker example, and externally, when shared with the outside world.

Now, I don't pretend to understand the scientific aspects of this critical and emotional thinking or the psychological process in which your thoughts bounce around in your head from your artistic and emotional right brain to your precise and logical left brain. While this is interesting and provides you with the analytical and internal process of the brain, your goal is simply to find out what time it is and not necessarily how the watch works.

Thoughts not only make you what you are; they can also make you what you want to be. Thoughts determine how you think, feel, how you live, and love. Thoughts become your ideas, and when transformed into your dreams, they become the action steps to your future world. Your memories are dedicated to the past, but your future is limited only by your thoughts and your imagination. When properly directed, your thoughts can provide a road map to achieving your goals. Thoughts are the beginning of a journey that, if directed, can change your life. You can't harvest the crops without first planting the seeds of thoughts in your mind.

Directed thoughts can be converted into your dreams, and eventually, when they are implemented into action, they can create your reality. As James Clear states in his book *Transform Your Habits*, "Reality creation is an inside job." Your thoughts create your reality. Your thoughts can take you on an exciting journey—they can multiply and explode into either a black hole or a fantastic world of possibilities.

Limitations live only in our minds, but if we use our imaginations, our possibilities become limitless.
—Jamie Paolinetti, writer and director of film, TV, and screenplays

You are today where your thoughts have brought you. You will be tomorrow where your thoughts take you.
—James Allen, New Zealand statesman

Thoughts without action are simply useless daydreams. You have the opportunity to convert your thoughts and dreams into a viable and meaningful plan with a little careful organization established in your game plan. You have some creative talents within your mind that you can call upon to implement and direct your thoughts, your beliefs, your feelings, your convictions, and your life. If you are what you do, if you are what you say, if you are what you think and know, then your thoughts become the basis of the actions that define you. So if you direct and control your thoughts, you direct and control your dreams and your life.

Watch your thoughts; they become words. Watch your words; they become actions. Watch your actions; they become habits. Watch your habits; they become character. Watch your character; it becomes your destiny.

—Frank Outlaw, founder of BI-LO supermarkets

Power of Thoughts

Thoughts are the product of your mind.
They are powerful, dangerous, and define.

You develop your inner self by what you think.
What you dream, feel, and say are all interlinked.

Carefully in control without destroying creative dreams,
Let your mind go crazy without knowing what it means.

Venture into this unknown world without fear.
As captain of your ship, your job is to steer.

Envision yourself as the star of the team.
Transfer your thoughts into your dream.

Thought becomes actions that make dreams come true—
Inspirational to watch and magical too.

—Morgan

Dream World

Dreams are the next phase of your thoughts. You have the power to transform your thoughts to dreams and transform your dreams to goals. You can accomplish your goals through carefully planned action steps. It's simple, it works, and you'll be able to confidently make it happen. It works for every aspect of your life.

You must define where you want to go, where you see yourself in the future, and what your future world will be. This creative process is fun, so set your mind free and dream the impossible so you might be what you want to be.

What is more important—thoughts or dreams? This question reminds me of a time when my wife and I were watching the Kentucky Derby, and I asked her, "What is more important, the horse or the jockey?"

As an expert horse person, she thought about it for a minute and said, "Both." This statement is equally true for thoughts and dreams. The difference between thoughts and dreams is a fine line. Dreams can't be created without thoughts, and our thoughts are useless without being incorporated into our dreams.

To dream anything that you want to dream, that's the beauty of the human mind. To do anything that you want to do, that is the strength of the human will. To trust yourself to test your limits is the courage to succeed.

—Bernard Edmonds, British clergyman

You must challenge your dreams. You must periodically leave your comfort zone and go beyond the familiar, and after a while, you will start feeling comfortable again.

Life begins at the end of your comfort zone.

—Neil Donald Walsh, author of Conversations with God

Kelly Clarkson's song "Breakaway" tells us, "I'll spread my wings, and I'll learn how to fly. I will make a wish, take a chance, make a change, and break away." You break away and venture into the unknown world of change. Take little steps, and before you know it, you'll learn to fly where only your dreams can take you.

Have confidence in your dreams, and don't let others influence what you can or can't do, because they have no idea about the power within you. You have but your own dreams to answer to, and you should not let outside negative forces interfere with your dreams. In many cases, dreamers are placed in the negative category: "You're just a dreamer," or "Don't fall in love with a dreamer." But dreaming is the most important step in the process of controlling and directing your thoughts and, ultimately, your life.

Recently, I read the book *Unchain the Elephant*, by Erik Wahl. The elephant, which is the largest animal on the Earth, is a magnificent and massive fourteen thousand pounds of raw power. In the wild, it is completely unrestrained and free to explore its world with very few restrictions. In captivity, however, baby elephants, which are 250–300 pounds, are chained to a tree or a stake to prevent them from escaping or wandering away. The baby elephants attempt to free themselves and test the strength of the chains constantly for the first few weeks of their lives in an attempt to secure freedom to explore the world around them. When they determine their efforts are no match for the heavy chains, they give up and accept the small circles that have been dictated to them. These restrictions are ingrained in the minds of the captive elephants forever, even as the power and strength they have attained as they grow could uproot that tree or post without much effort.

You need to break the chains that bind you so that you have the freedom to explore your world without the restrictions of your past. Unshackle those chains, and do not allow those outside influences dictate what you can or can't do.

Create your dream plan, seek advice, and learn, but always follow your dreams. Be as specific as possible: "Not only do I want to improve my golf game, but I also want my handicap to be 9.5 by August 1." As Regina Belle says in her song, "When I dream, I dream in color." You likely face the challenges that many of us face—not determining *how* to achieve your goals, but rather what your hopes and dreams *are*. Find those things that you are passionate about.

Many things will catch your eye, but few will catch your heart. . . pursue those.

—Michael Nolan, United Kingdom judge

This creative progression requires you to search deep in your soul for those things that inspire you. Maybe it's as simple as identifying those people you admire. Ask yourself, "What am I good at?" or "What do I really enjoy doing?" The process will have its drawbacks. Some things you try may not work, but I can guarantee that nothing will work unless you try. You will sometimes be wrong. There are times when you will come up against an immovable hurdle, so you need to determine if there are ways around these obstacles. It's amazing how, when you go down a path and when your experiences allow you to discover new ideas, you meet new people and find fresh ways to achieve your dreams. Sometimes you will need to review and adjust your direction, as success is not a straight line. Failure is not permanent, and in many cases, it's not necessarily a bad thing. Sometimes we learn more from our mistakes than we could ever learn from our successes.

Experience is the name everyone gives their mistakes.
—Oscar Wilde, Irish author and playwright

Let me tell you a personal story about one of my dreams and how, after years of hard work, I fell short of achieving my goal. The lessons learned through my journey far exceeded the disappointments.

Like many children growing up, I loved sports. I played high-school football, along with one million one hundred thousand other kids. As quarterback for our high-school state-championship team, I dreamed of playing in Division I college football—maybe twelve thousand other athletes were able to also achieve that same dream, which made my probability of success somewhere around 1 percent.

My ultimate goal was to play professional football in the NFL, which, at that time, had fewer than eight hundred players and drafted maybe 200 players each year, providing me with an unrealistic 5,500 to 1 shot at being able to achieve my dreams. I was not to be deterred, and my dream continued as I went on to Michigan State, where we were Big Ten champions and national champions for two years (1965 and 1966). During my senior year, four of the top eight players drafted by the NFL came from my graduating class. Fifteen players from my team went on to play at the professional level, and I was not one of them. Four of those players are now in the Football Hall of Fame.

While I was an integral part of this team, I was only able to achieve the status of backup quarterback. But an interesting thing happened during those four years: I reached what I called the "Peter Principle" of my athletic career, which means I grew to my height of athletic incompetence, as the talent pool at Big Ten levels was the best of the best. Dr. Lawrence Peters, a Canadian educator and sociologist in his book *The Peter Principle*, describes the bureaucratic theory that employees within an organization advance to their highest level of competence and eventually are promoted to their level of incompetence. It was great to be part of that experience, and it was a wonderful way to go out. My dreams may have fallen short of my expectations, but I will forever cherish the life lessons I learned: the teamwork necessary to be successful; the hard work; the dedication to my goals; the importance of knowing the strengths, weakness, and limitations of my opponents as well as my own; and the leadership abilities needed to succeed. My education was not all achieved in the classroom.

The point is that failure doesn't have to be a setback as long as we adapt and learn from those disappointments. The positive kernels of knowledge this process has given me—plus the talents and insight that I learned and have utilized throughout my life—are far more valuable than my failure to achieve my goal of playing in the NFL. The truth is that either way, I was the winner.

If you can find a path with no obstacles, it probably doesn't lead anywhere.

—Frank A. Clark, American writer and cartoonist

These invaluable lessons are transferable, and you need to know they are life's way of telling you that sometimes you don't win them all. Opportunities present themselves to those who are busy, active, and focused—those who realize that success is not a straight line. Be aware that when you take control of your life, you become the benefactor of your thoughts and dreams. The mind is a powerful instrument that crystallizes strategies, harbors ambitions, visualizes plans, creates hope, and establishes direction.

Dreams aren't realized by simply dreaming. Dreams are realized by carefully converting your dream planning to action steps after you've dreamed them:

1. Thoughts to dreams
2. Dreams to goals
3. Goals to action steps
4. Action steps to reality—or you are just wasting your time

Calculated dreamtime has no borders or boundaries. We all possess dream power, and there is no limit to how ideas can be transformed into reality.

There are some people who live in a dream world, and there are some who face reality; and then there are those who turn one into the other.

—Douglas Everett, Canadian senator and attorney

Some dreams require a massive amount effort to achieve—but don't let this scare you. To conceive your dream world you need to let the boundaries of your imagination go wild, as nothing is impossible.

A few years back, looking out from the patio of my condo in Chicago, I could see an ADIDAS billboard that utilized a quote from Muhammad Ali.

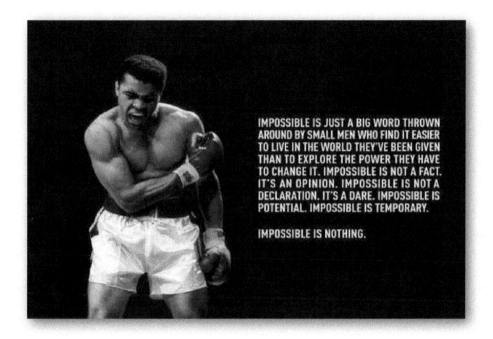

IMPOSSIBLE IS JUST A BIG WORD THROWN AROUND BY SMALL MEN WHO FIND IT EASIER TO LIVE IN THE WORLD THEY'VE BEEN GIVEN THAN TO EXPLORE THE POWER THEY HAVE TO CHANGE IT. IMPOSSIBLE IS NOT A FACT. IT'S AN OPINION. IMPOSSIBLE IS NOT A DECLARATION. IT'S A DARE. IMPOSSIBLE IS POTENTIAL. IMPOSSIBLE IS TEMPORARY.

IMPOSSIBLE IS NOTHING.

History indicates that, in the athletic track world, a sub-four-minute mile was considered impossible and even dangerous by physiologists prior to Roger Bannister's historical, record-breaking feat on May 6, 1954, when he ran a 3-minute, 59.4-second mile. Once the psychological barrier was broken, the floodgates opened, and this record was broken by the Australian athlete John Landy just forty-six days later. It's estimated that there have been over 1,100 sub-four-minute miles recorded since that historic accomplishment. The current record of 3 minutes, 43.13 seconds solidifies that "Impossible is nothing," and if you can dream it, you can achieve it.

Without dreams, you are hopelessly stuck in reality TV. Without dreams, you are destined to live in a world made up of black and white. Without dreams, there is no ambition, only mindless actions.

As Kenny Rogers song says, "Don't Fall in Love with a Dreamer," but my wish for you is that you will become a dreamer, fall desperately in love with a dreamer, and lay it out there every day and in every way possible.

Live out every dream and hold on to the excitement—the thrill of winning without hesitation or fear of not making your dreams come true.

Our doubts are our traitors, and make us lose the good we oft might win by fearing to attempt

—William Shakespeare

Don't let temporary failures be a deterrent to dreams, as failure only makes those dreams that come true even more powerful and fulfilling. To dream and fail is a hundred times better than to never dream at all. Dreams require belief in yourself. Dreams require commitment. Dream every dream in Technicolor, on the big screen of your minds.

Dream World

The quiet dream voice inside your head is a valuable jewel.
It's creative, it's limitless, and it's a powerful tool.

Your dream world has very few restrictions.
It's void of barriers, of rules and predictions.

You dream in color and avoid black and white.
The blank canvas is yours, and you paint what you like.

Nothing is impossible if you can dream it to be.
You can make it happen, and believing is the key.

You search your soul, tap your passion, and take it far.
Take control of your life and raise the bar.

Your dreams transform and crystallize your direction.
As benefactor of your dreams, you search for perfection.

Set aside the time to evaluate where you are.
Determine your path and how to become a star.

Dream no small dreams as you reach for the moon.
As you attempt the unthinkable, it will happen soon.

Get out the crystal ball to determine where you want to go,
And paint the picture as if you were Vincent Van Gogh.

Follow your dreams shown in the art,
As it becomes the passion of your heart

—Morgan

COURAGE OF CHANGE

Change involves risks, but without risk you can never change.

Sometimes, you need to go out onto that limb, take that risk, and venture into the unknown so you might experience the joys of change. If you are happy with your life, if you are satisfied with the cards you've been dealt, keep doing whatever you're doing, as you are where we all want to be. But if you're not happy with your situation, it's time to take that risk and make that change! I love Albert Einstein's quote about insanity.

Insanity: doing the same thing over and over again and expecting different results.

—Albert Einstein

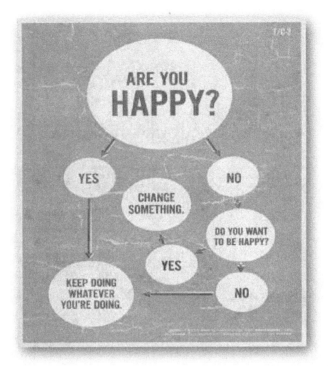

My wish for you is that you will not be afraid to dream or love, and when you get the chance...to dance. Taking chances is sometimes hard and sometimes painful. Doors open and doors close—waiting to hear, "I love you, too." But, not to dance is to settle or give in to the path of least resistance, and that is just sad.

The excitement of youth, as described in Lee Ann Womack's song "I Hope You Dance"—"When you get the chance, I hope you choose to dance"—gives you hope that you and your children and your children's children will never lose that sense of wonder. And when they get the chance to sit it out or dance...you hope they dance.

Take risk! If you win, you will be happy. If you lose, you will be wise.
—Unknown

As you get older, some of the biggest regrets you'll have will be those things you didn't do. The easiest avenue to avoid risk and change is always *no*—and certainly *no* is an option, and sometimes *no* is the appropriate choice. You just need to make sure you are not selecting *no* because of the fear of change or failure, the amount of effort required to change, or the fear of venturing into the unknown.

Imperfect action is better than perfect inaction.
—Harry Truman, thirty-third president of the United States

Life is change. Growth is optional. Choose wisely.
—Karen Kaiser Clark, motivational speaker

In the long run, however, sameness is the fast track to mediocrity, and mediocrity can't survive. Leaving your comfort zone, which you have spent years perfecting, always requires more effort, more risk, but if you want to grow, you need to leave your existing world to progress to the next level. You either get better or you get worse; you never stay the same.

When patterns are broken, new worlds emerge.
—Tuli Kupferberg, American poet and author of Counter Culture

And that is your challenge: to convince yourself that the new world you are trying to create is better than the one you have built for yourself. Is it easy? Of course not...It takes planning, commitment, patience, and courage.

Not everything that is faced can be changed, but nothing can be changed unless it's faced.

—James Baldwin, American writer, playwright, and poet

The truth, of course, is that change can be a wonderful gift. In fact, it's the key that unlocks the doors to growth and excitement in your life. Without change, possibilities and opportunities will pass you by. You must take the risk and grab the brass ring so that the accumulation of your personal kernels of knowledge never stops.

Behold the turtle. He makes progress only when he sticks his neck out

—James Bryant Conant, chemist and past president of Harvard University

You have a precious streak of brilliance with built-in capabilities, and you just need to find it, encourage it, and use it. A big part of success is getting out of your world of sameness and taking that calculated risk to assure yourself that, even though you are on a new path, it's the right path, for the right reasons.

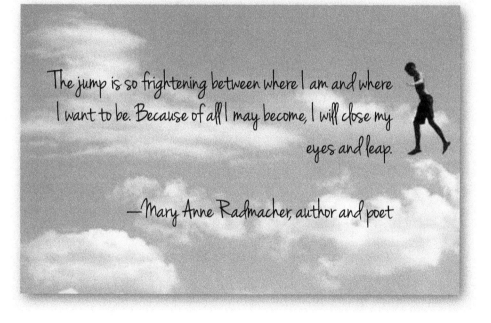

The jump is so frightening between where I am and where I want to be. Because of all I may become, I will close my eyes and leap.

—Mary Anne Radmacher, author and poet

Courage of Change

Venture into the unknown world of change.
Give your life the courage to rearrange.

You either get better or worse, but never stay the same.
So dedicate your efforts to improve your game.

You have three strikes, so use them all.
Don't give up and keep your eye on the ball.

You learn from your mistakes, so don't be afraid to try.
When you step out into the unknown, you learn to fly.

—Morgan

Success Is Not a Straight Line

You venture into this world with great hopes and dreams, and sometimes they are realized and sometimes not. The ones that work are a lot more fun. The setbacks you experience are harder to accept, but you must realize if they were all successful, the joy of winning would not be the same. We all experience setbacks, but the important thing is how we handle them. You can crawl in a hole and feel sorry for yourself, or you can hit Ctrl+Alt+Delete and start again.

"If it was easy, anyone could do it," as the saying goes. I like the story about Ray Kroc, the founder of McDonald's. He spent years attempting to raise the capital needed to launch the McDonald's restaurant chain. He had a very humble beginning, with a number of menial jobs and financial difficulties because of several failed enterprises. He was fifty-two years old when he was finally able to convince enough people to invest in what many called a "crazy" idea. But in the end, he was able to amass a family fortune that is estimated at $1.7 billion, with 33,000 stores located in 118 countries. His success was mainly due to his persistence and dedication to changing how the world viewed the restaurant business.

Adversity is a state of mind in which man most easily becomes acquainted with himself.

—John Wooden, UCLA basketball coach

If it is true that we learn from our mistakes, I must be pretty smart, because I've done so many dumb things. If you want to try to find that pot of gold at the end of the rainbow, you need to conquer your fears, take that risk, leave your comfort zone, and just do it! You do not want to ever have to make the statement, "I wish I had…"

Good judgment is the result of experience and experience the result of bad judgment.

—Mark Twain

Some people think success is luck, but you know better. To be successful, the important thing is to keep swinging and keep getting back up to bat. It's not how many home runs you hit but rather how many times you get back up and try.

Babe Ruth hit 714 home runs during his career. By most standards, he was one of the all-time greatest baseball players. He was a baseball legend, but what you might not know is that he also led the league in strikeouts for five seasons. He struck out 1,330 times in his career. He had an amazing lifetime batting average of .342, which means he failed almost seven out of ten times. I love Babe Ruth's attitude about trying.

Never let the fear of striking out get in your way.

—Babe Ruth

As Jack Canfield explains in his book, *The Success Principles*, when he and Mark Victor Hansen were attempting to find a publisher for their book *Chicken Soup for the Soul* after over 144 rejections, a small, struggling publisher headed by Peter Vergo and Gary Seidler agreed to publish their book. The book went on to sell over ten million copies and created a spin-off series of 225 best-selling books that have been translated in forty-seven languages.

The individual who fails but gets back up and continues to try will eventually get the deal, make the sale, win the heart of that special person, and be more successful.

Courage doesn't always roar. Sometimes courage is the little voice at the end of the day that says, "I'll try again tomorrow."

—Mary Radmacher, American author and poet

Persistence tied with mediocre talent will win the majority of the time against the more talented person who gives up because he or she fails seven out of ten times. True greatness is achieved when talent and persistence meet. As proof that success is not a straight line, Michael Jordon—a skinny kid from Laney High School who was cut from the basketball team as a sophomore—would have never achieved the status of being one of the greatest basketball players of all time had it not been for his persistence.

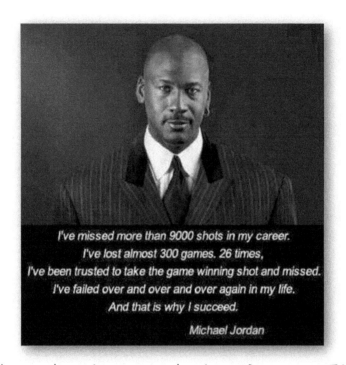

I've missed more than 9000 shots in my career.
I've lost almost 300 games. 26 times,
I've been trusted to take the game winning shot and missed.
I've failed over and over and over again in my life.
And that is why I succeed.

Michael Jordan

Nothing in the world can take the place of Persistence. Talents will not; nothing is more common than unsuccessful men with talent. Genius will not; unrewarded genius is almost a proverb. Education will not; the world is full of educated derelicts. Persistence and determination alone are omnipotent.

—Calvin Coolidge, thirtieth president of the United States

Success is not a straight line.

Your world is full of hopes and dreams.
Nothing is what it first seems.

Persistence is the key to achieving success.
Greatness is realized as you progress.

Some say intelligence, and others say megabucks.
Some say breaks, and some say just luck.

No one succeeds without mistakes,
Without pain and suffering and heartaches.

If the pot of gold is to be redeemed,
Persistence holds the key to achieving your dreams.

Our road to happiness we strive to find,
And we realize that success is not a straight line.

—Morgan

FEAR IS MY FRIEND

THE EMOTIONS OF fear are healthy. Fear is created to assure that you use caution, but facing your fears is the first step to their elimination. Fear of the unknown, if not faced, if not analyzed, addressed, and conquered, causes the death of dreams. Conquering your fears requires venturing into the unknown, but when faced, fears become the lessons you've mastered. When limitations—caused by your fears—are overcome, a new world presents itself.

Inaction breeds doubt and fear. Action breeds confidence and courage. If you want to conquer fear, do not sit home and think about it. Go out and get busy.
—Dale Carnegie, writer, lecturer, and the developer of the famous Dale Carnegie Institute

You need to address your fears head on and take control, as fear becomes the opportunity for change. The confidence you'll achieve by facing these flashes of fear will enable you to experience, identify, and become familiar with methods of solving issues. Fears conquered become assets rather than liabilities and limitations. The confidence and character you'll build by facing your fears is directly proportionate to the number of times you look fear in the face. Once familiar with your fears, you'll understand them, and once you understand them, they can no longer paralyze your dreams.

Do the thing we fear, and death of fear is certain.
—Ralph Waldo Emerson

I am not saying we can totally eliminate all our fears, as they are valuable assets that make us far more successful, with happier results. Fear requires you to double check the numbers, use caution in that special romance, or think twice before you say "yes." You just need to realize that to reach that pot of gold at the end of the rainbow, you must address and overcome your fears.

We fear things in proportion to our ignorance of them.
—Titus Livius, Roman historian

Remember when you first learned to swim? Remember the fear of taking that first jump into the deep end of the pool? No water wings, no life jacket—just you and the ten-foot-deep water. Did someone have to shove you? After that first leap, the fear turned into excitement, joy, and fun.

You realized that all the anxiety you built up in your mind was nothing! Your entire life you'll face and eliminate one fear after another, just like learning to swim. You conquer your fears one at a time, and while it may not always be exciting and fun, doing so will teach you that, through that door of fear, opportunity presents itself.

The cave you fear to enter holds the treasure you seek.
—Joseph Campbell, American writer and lecturer

I have been an entrepreneur for most of my life, and I have to admit that even now, the fear of failure looms large on my radar. I'll never forget when, in 1998, I was president of the urban division of a large, publicly traded real-estate development company, and the board of directors decided to sell off my division. After a great deal of deliberation, I decided to take a scary step and venture out into the real-estate development world *alone* and start my own company. I had spent years paying my dues, and it required a great deal of money and risk to start my own company. The fear of taking that step into the unknown, the fear of failure, the fear and risk of losing money, the fear that if I failed everything I'd worked for all my life would be destroyed—it was real. But I looked fear in the face and took the leap. The hurdles were huge, but when I was successful, so were the rewards.

When we face fear, experience it, we not only diminish that fear but also increase our confidence, even if we're not successful, and just the fact that we faced our fears makes all fears more manageable.

I have faced my fears many times and continue to do so every day. Fear is real, and I respect it. I am even starting to understand it. On occasion, fear has actually hurt me. If you want to respect fear, try losing money and you will pay more attention next time. I was fortunate as I experienced the "thrill of victory" more than the "agony of defeat"—success is not a straight line. But even when the worst happens, you realize that your fears won't eat you. Failure hurts but also teaches you valuable lessons.

I've never counted the number of my fears, but I can tell you there are fewer now than a few years ago. As you address your fears and either eliminate or negate their power, you become more confident. When even one fear is eliminated, your comfort zone is expanded, and you increase your options and your freedom.

Now, the title of this chapter is "Fear Is My Friend," and I must admit that this is a little overstated. It's certainly not my best friend, but it is one I know intimately, and we understand each other very well. Fear sometimes is developed through experience, and I have seen the good and the bad, so I always invite my "fear of failure person" to my personal Meeting with Myself. He or she has great judgment, and I have learned to address this person's concerns.

So, sometimes you do not eliminate your fears, but you learn to live with them. The interesting thing about fear is that once it's conquered, it vanishes, or at least you diminish its power forever. So, yes, fear is my friend.

Ultimately we know deeply that the other side of every fear is freedom.

—Marilyn Ferguson, an American writer

Character can't be developed in ease and quiet. Only through experiences of trial and suffering can the soul be strengthened, vision cleared, ambition inspired, and success achieved.

—Helen Keller

Fear Is My Friend

Fear is scary and gets your attention fast
If not faced head on, it will forever last.

Fear of failure is your worst nightmare,
And the courage to fight is your dare.

Battle your fear, as it is a destroyer of dreams.
Conquer your fear with actions that redeem.

Fear is a great motivator in many ways.
With time and hard work, dividends it pays.

Knowledge and preparation combat your fears.
Face each of them head on as they appear.

If mistakes and corrections are needed to mend,
Listen and remember as. . .fear is my friend.

—Morgan

I Believe I Can Fly

Armed with only talent, ambition, and the dedication and belief that they could create the worlds of their dreams, the individuals in the following stories have overcome their limitations, have taken that leap into the unknown, and have learned how to fly. They will help you to understand the power you have within you to believe in yourself, to reach for the stars, and to develop the attitude and belief that, although you may face hurdles, you *can* overcome setbacks and you *can* accomplish anything.

These individuals all started with nothing other than a strong belief that they could fly! Your success will be assured through not only intelligence, money, drive, ambition, talent, desire, hard work, but the *belief* that *you* can truly fly.

The moment of enlightenment is when a person's dreams of possibili-
ties become images of probabilities.
—Vic Braden, American tennis player and broadcaster

THE KID FROM DETROIT

In the mid-1990s, I hired and mentored a young man from the depths of Detroit to handle a 150-unit warehouse-loft condominium conversion located in the River North neighborhood of Chicago. David was fresh out of the University of Michigan—a bright, ambitious young man with talent. He was involved in the sales and marketing of this development, which he presold within the first ninety days! This was an incredible accomplishment, even though it took us about eighteen months to construct and close out the community.

He went on to establish a partnership with a couple of similarly ambitious, talented young men who founded one of the largest real-estate brokerage companies in the Midwest. They thought they could fly and set out to conquer the world—and they did.

David frequently talked about his dream of creating a luxury hotel, the likes of which even Chicago had never seen. And he eventually went on to develop the Elysian Hotel, a $200 million, five-star, fifty-four-story hotel and condominium located in the center of the world—on Walton Street in Chicago. He eventually sold the Elysian Hotel; it's now known as the Waldorf Astoria Chicago. Recently, these luxurious condominiums have resold in the $8–10 million range.

David is a prime example of an individual who believed in his dreams. And he continues to expand and achieve his dreams. It's been fun to watch him and to have played a small part in seeing him become "more than he thought he could be"—although I'd be willing to wager that David still thinks he hasn't lived that dream yet.

The future belongs to those who believe in the beauty of their dreams.

—Eleanor Roosevelt

SUPER GOR

Another close friend of mine, with whom I played football at Michigan State, is a great example of talented determination partnered with nothing but a firm belief that he could fly. Gor was from Oak Park, Illinois, and was a great athlete, having played both football and basketball at a Big Ten level, which is an incredible accomplishment in itself. He took his humble beginnings, as the son of a Chicago policeman, to a level most of us can only imagine. He believed in himself, and he always had a passion for what he was doing. His vision was extraordinary, and he believed he could fly.

After several years of focused and well-calculated risks, he has achieved far more than just money. Gor accumulated diversified business holdings in real estate, banking, and manufacturing; he owns several companies all over the world and has a wonderful family and a beautiful second home in Florida. He also generously supports and is active in charities, as well as serving as director of the Michigan State University Foundation. Now, here is a self-made man who started with nothing but talent and belief in his dreams. He not only believed he could fly; he does it quite often—all around the world in his private jet.

Champions aren't made in the gyms. Champions are made from something they have deep inside them—a desire, a dream, a vision.

—Muhammad Ali

ONE PUTT

I heard a story about a golfer who had been having problems with his putting game all season long. Then one day, he was on the putting green, draining fifteen footers one after another, and his playing partner asked, "What happened?"

He said, "It's my new magic ball. The club professional gave it to me. It's new; the Titleist representative just gave it to him. It's perfectly balanced, with special dimples and a built-in radar that just zeroes in on the hole."

Now, the ball was a normal golf ball and had no special powers, but the golfer thought it was magic, and the results were extraordinary. The lesson is that the power of our beliefs are real, and if we believe we are going to sink that putt, make that deal, or win the heart of that special person, chances are much better that we will.

Mr. Franchise

My high-school and Michigan State teammate and very good friend Phil was a 215-pound starting defensive end on our national-championship football team. He was the other end from Bubba Smith—a six-foot-eight, 310-pound all-American—so the other teams liked to try and run Phil's way (away from the "Kill, Bubba, kill!" chants of the seventy-five thousand fans in the stadium). Phil had learned early on the determination and guts in his beliefs, and they have served him well throughout his career.

Phil was a very successful football player and, after graduation, a successful entrepreneur. He owns over seventy-five Burger Kings and Qdoba restaurant franchises throughout the East Coast. Phil is an honorary faculty member at the Michigan State Hospitality School, where he is affectionately known as "the Emperor." He is another great example of an ordinary talent who was elevated to greatness through his extraordinary belief in his ability to fly.

Yours Truly, Morgan

After years of paying my dues for, and being mentored by, the largest Chicago condominium developers in the late 1980s to mid-1990s, I was approached, in 1994, by a large publicly traded homebuilder to head up a division in downtown Chicago. It was the most professionally prolific and magical time for the "deal junkie" in me, as it provided the financial backing to fulfill a lifetime dream of recruiting and assembling the best and the brightest, providing them with my vision, and orchestrating the process. We believed there wasn't anything we couldn't do, as we successfully coordinated several developments projects with over $150 million in sales within a four-year period. We believed we could fly—and we did!

A single thread runs through all of these success stories: a firm "I believe I can fly" attitude. Not money, not fame, not extraordinary intelligence—just a burning desire and belief that "if I can dream it, I can achieve it, and I have the courage to try it!"

When you walk to the edge of all the light, you have to take that first step into the darkness of the unknown. You must believe that one of two things will happen: there will be something solid for you to stand on or you will be taught to fly.

—Patrick Overton, minister, teacher, and poet

I THINK I CAN

I used to read my kids a book titled *The Little Engine That Could*, originally authored by Francis Ford and later published under the name Watty Piper. The story is about a big steam engine that breaks down while attempting to transport toys to a city just over the mountain in time for Christmas. After several attempts—with no success—to get help from the big, powerful engines that come along, a cute little engine comes by and says, "Sure, I'll help you." But she's not really sure she can do it.

As this little engine hooks up to the stranded train and starts to chug up the mountain, it becomes increasingly more difficult, and she keeps saying to herself, "I think I can—I think I can—I think I can." It becomes harder and harder as she climbs the mountain. But as her confidence grows and she gets closer to the top, the little engine starts to chug faster and faster until she reaches the top of the mountain. Then she says to herself, "I thought I could. I thought I could. I thought I could." The train delivers the toys, and the children enjoyed their presents.

Now, there are many lessons to be learned in this story. First, you get great joy and contentment in helping others. But also, unfortunately, a lot of people don't care about your problems—they've got their own to deal with. The most important lesson of all is that you should never give up; you don't know what you might accomplish unless you try, and you may just determine that you can fly!

The power you have within yourself and the determination you've set out for yourself to accomplish your goals—just as the engine learned—are achieved one step at a time. Your confidence grows with each step, and as your confidence grows, you get closer to achieving your dreams.

I Believe I Can Fly

Conventional wisdom states, "I'll believe it when I can see it." But the absolute, unwavering, and indisputable principles of universal law clearly state, "Unless and until you *believe* it, you will *not* see it."

This book contains great kernels of knowledge that you can utilize by crawling inside yourself to determine what you want out of life and what methods you want to use to achieve them. I have used all these methods, and I have proven to myself that the principles work. But *none* of them will work unless *you* dedicate *yourself* and believe *you* can accomplish *your* dreams. Or, as R. Kelly says in his song, "If I can see it, then I can do it. If I just believe it. Then there's nothing to it. I believe I can fly."

I Believe I Can Fly

Confidence starts one baby step at a time.
Soon, there won't be a mountain you can't climb.

You face your challenges every day
With the belief you can fly away.

You develop your beliefs and eliminate your fear,
As your direction and goals become crystal clear.

You will not be afraid of anything new,
As there is nothing you can't do.

You jump into the darkness and continue to try.
Greatness can be achieved, as I believe I can fly.

—Morgan

Recommended Reading

Scientific Books

Sometimes, while writing this book, I had to stop and shake the hayseeds out of my hair. I found some incredible scientific data from experts who know a lot more about the inner workings of the mind than I could have ever imagined. But interestingly, they have proven that the practical conclusions I have developed over my lifetime are actually supported by scientific evidence. Therefore, I submit the following books and articles as references to help you to determine not only what time it is but also how the watch works.

The Power of the Subconscious Mind, by Dr. Joseph Murphy
www.ichoosetoheal.com/.../**the-power-of-your-subconscious-mind.pdf**
This book offers a practical guide to understanding and learning to use the incredible powers you possess within you. It gives you the tools you will need to unlock the awesome powers of your subconscious mind.

Thought Power—Your Thoughts Create Your Reality, by Tania Kotsos
www.mind-**your-reality**.com/**thought_power**.html
Thought power is the key to creating your reality. Everything you perceive in the physical world has its origin in the invisible, inner world of your thoughts and beliefs. To become the master of your destiny, you must learn to control the nature of your dominant habitual thoughts. Tania Kotsos has written several insightful articles that deal with thoughts and the conversion of these thoughts into our reality.

The Adventure of I, by Tania Kotsos
www.mind-your-reality.com/**the_adventure**_of_I.html
This is one of the most complete, logical, and practical books written about the power of the human mind, universal consciousness, the laws and principles of the universe, and your ability to direct your mind and create the life you desire with the power of your will. This book will take you on a journey to the center of your reality, where you will discover the mighty "I" within, and in so doing, you will come to understand just what is meant by the greatest maxim of all time, "Know thyself."

Some of Tania Kotsos's other works include the following:
Law of Attraction Demystified
Self-Love—the Greatest Love of All
Creative Visualization Demystified
Mind Your Reality (www.mind-your-reality.com)

Power of Thought—a Quantum Perspective, by Kent Healy
www.mrnice.nl/.../13403-**power-thought-quantum-perspective**.html
This book presents a scientific approach to explaining the power of thought. We have all heard it before: "Your thoughts create your reality." Well, new quantum-physics studies support this idea. Learn about recent research into how the mind can influence the behavior of subatomic particles and physical matter.

The Secret, by Rhonda Byrne
thesecretrhondabyrne.com
This book reveals how you can change every aspect of your life. You can turn any weakness or suffering into strength, power, unlimited abundance, health, and joy. Everything is possible; nothing is impossible. There are no limits. Whatever you can dream of can be yours when you use "the secret."

Mindsight: The New Science of Personal Transformation, by Dr. Daniel Siegel
www.**drdansiegel**.com/books/**mindsight**

Leading neurobiologist Dr. Daniel J. Siegel's book on the healing power of "mindsight," the potent skill that is the basis for both emotional and social intelligence, allows you to make positive changes in your brain and in your life.

"Second Wave of Transformation," by John Mauldin
www.**mauldin**economics.com/frontlinethoughts/**the-age-of-trans formation**

This article gives us some insight into our future world, both personal and financial. Mauldin explores these multiple and rapidly accelerating changes happening simultaneously that are going to transform our social structures, our investment portfolios, and our personal futures. Everything from nanotechnology and medical science to solar energy—you name it. He evaluates how it will transform our future world.

MOTIVATIONAL BOOKS

WHEN SCIENTIFIC EVIDENCE is combined with the emotional power we have within us, the combination is exponentially powerful.

The Success Principles, by Jack Canfield
www.**thesuccessprinciples**.com

It has been hailed as the new self-improvement classic, containing sixty-seven of the most powerful principles of success known to humankind. Since its publication a decade ago, Jack Canfield's practical and inspiring guide has helped thousands of people transform themselves for success.

Chicken Soup for the Soul, by Jack Canfield and Mark Victor Hansen
www.barnesandnoble.com/w/**chicken-soup-for-the-christian-soul-jack**...

This book is an accumulation of stories that will motivate, teach, make you laugh, inspire you, and provide nutritional recipes to rekindle your spirit. The original *Chicken Soup for the Soul* has inspired a series of 225 books that are now published in forty-seven languages.

Unchain the Elephant, by Erik Wahl
*www.amazon.com/***Unchain-Elephant**.

This describes an interesting analogy between an elephant in the wild and an elephant in captivity and makes it clear that we need to break the chains that bind us so that we have the freedom to explore our world without the restrictions of our past.

To a Child Love Is Spelled T-I-M-E, by Mac Anderson and Lance Wubbels
*www.nightingale.com/***child-love-is-spelled**-*t-i-m-e.html*

This is an inspiring book that will take you about twenty minutes to read but can change your relationships with your children and your children's children forever.

The Little Engine That Could, by Francis Ford and Watty Piper
https://en.wikipedia.org/wiki/The_Little_Engine_That_Could
This is a fun children's book filled with great lessons for all of us.

Inspirational Songs

THIS IS A list of inspirational songs, all of which are mentioned in this book, that have had a motivational effect on me. Now, my children call it "elevator music," and I have come to learn that music is a very personal choice. My advice to them, as well as to you, is to find your own "elevator," as the inspirational impact can be amazing.

"Breakaway," by Kelly Clarkson
"I Believe I Can Fly," by R. Kelly
"I Hope You Dance," by Lee Ann Womack
"One Moment in Time," by Whitney Houston
"Don't Fall in Love with a Dreamer", by Kenny Rogers

You're off to great places!
Today is your day!
Your mountain is waiting,
So get on your way.
—Dr. Seuss

May these kernels of knowledge serve you well.
Follow the advice, and only time will tell.
The principles are simple if you only try.
Good luck as it's time to say good-bye.

—Morgan

ABOUT THE AUTHOR

JOHN MORGAN MULLEN owns a real estate development and consulting company specializing in urban infill, adaptive reuse, historic renovations, and community development properties. Morgan has played a major role in the warehouse loft conversion boom and gentrification of many Chicago neighborhoods valued at over $600 million.

Morgan attended Michigan State University, where he earned a BA in communication arts. He was a quarterback for Michigan State University on two National Championship teams in 1965 and 1966. Morgan credits athletics for honing and developing his dedication to hard work, leadership, teamwork, developing a game plan, and knowing your opponent's strengths and weaknesses as well as your own.

Married to his college sweetheart Jill for forty-eight years, Morgan has two children, Todd and Stephanie. He and Jill are grandparents to Jake, Brennan, and Hailey.

More information on Morgan's professional life is available at www.morgangroupdev.com.

CPSIA information can be obtained
at www.ICGtesting.com
Printed in the USA
LVHW031012181218
600843LV00015B/911/P